Homeless at Age 13 to a College Graduate

AN AUTOBIOGRAPHY

ANTHONY DEVONTA ROSS

Anthony D. Ross

ISBN: 0991322436
ISBN-13: 9780991322435

This book is dedicated to my grandmother Ethel Hight. May your beautiful spirit continue to live on through the gates of Heaven. And to the LeTendre Scholars from the National Association for the Education of Homeless Children and Youth Class of 2009: Lexie Merill, Danielle Loster, Patrick Ma, Samantha Gardner, Lace King, Stephanie Schafer, Timothy Bethune, Jessica White, and the rest, may you all continue to soar for excellence and inspire the people around you.

"Somewhere inside all of us is the power to change the world."

-Inspired by the motion picture *Matilda*

Contents

Chapter One

A Childhood of Hidden Love

GO TO YOUR ROOM!" my grandmother yelled. This was where I spent most of my days as a child. In my room staring at the four walls in solitude and curiosity as to why I always spent much of my time in this lonely box. However, someday, my question was soon answered. As a child, my grandmother would always tell me the story of her having to pick me up from crack houses as an infant because it was where my mother would spend most of her life. Living in northeast Washington, D.C. in a house with three older sisters with me being the only boy, I wondered why my life was the way it was: Fatherless and an absent mother as my grandmother served as our guardian.

While growing up, my sisters always received favoritism from my grandmother. Whenever I did something wrong, my punishment was usually more severe than theirs. Being locked away in my room and deprived from eating for days was very challenging for me because I never understood why I received such harsh treatment at such a young age but had to accept it because it became normal to me. During the days that I wasn't allowed to eat any food, my cousin would sometimes slip granola bars under my bedroom door to keep me from starving but it did not prevent the accumulation of stomach ulcers and other ailments caused by the suffering. The suffering intensified when I only saw my mother three days out of a year either showing up late for my birthday or nowhere to be found on Christmas day.

As I began to grow older, her absence no longer affected me as much because I became used to it. During the times spent in my room alone on punishment, I despised God and always asked him why. "Why me? Why did I have to be born into this family? God, I hate you!" I would yell crying myself to sleep several nights wishing my last name was different from everyone else in my family. There even were times where my oldest sister intervened during sessions where my grandmother would beat on me for hours. "Stop hitting him like that!" my oldest sister would yell as the beatings intensified but this was just another normal day for me because my body got used to the punishment.

On some days when I was not being punished, I would watch television and hear the sound of the doorbell. As I walked to the door, I would see older males and try to decipher which ones could be my father hoping that one day the man that will be my father will arrive at the door step; however, that hope remained afloat. As dark clouds grew and the moon started to glow, my childhood was gone with the wind; imagining the joys and happiness that life could bring. From all of the suffering and malicious punishments endured, my teenage years began to approach swiftly wishing that I had experienced a normal childhood like my peers in pre-k and elementary school. It was not until after my 13th birthday that my life took a course of unexpected events.

Chapter Two

A Twist of Fate

As I thought my life would be made of endless suffering and punishment, something unexpected happened that even the family could not predict; the death of my grandmother. At age 13, I lost my grandmother to heart disease who was the sole guardian of my sisters and me. I did not understand death at the time. All I could hear from my aunts and mom is that my grandmother passed on to a better place. Even though my aunts and uncles would always tell me that I was abused and mistreated as a child by her, I felt as if I never received the opportunity to really get to know who she really was. At the time of her death, the family began to think of where my sisters and I were going to live. During this time, my mother made the decision to step up and be the mother that she never was. She vowed to take care of us, enroll us into school, and make a better life for us. I was very excited when I saw my mother while growing up; even when she arrived late to my birthdays empty handed. So for my sisters and I to finally live with her put smiles on our faces.

Days after my grandmother's death, my sisters and I began to make a new life in Upper Marlboro, Maryland living with our mom. Meeting new friends and living in the same house with my little sister helped us love life a lot more. However, the days of enjoying a better life passed swiftly and the suffering that I endured while living with my grandmother began to haunt me yet once again. "Who touched this? Did you do this?" were common questions my mother would wake us in the middle of the night asking. With my sisters knowing that something was happening to our mom, we began to believe that something was starting to take over her soul. During the summertime, my sisters and I would go to Six Flags theme park with some friends in the neighborhood to get away from the negativity at home. My sisters and I would discuss that we noticed strange things happening to our mother and tried to figure out exactly what it was. It was only until nine months after my grandmother died that our lives were not actually becoming better as we thought but started to become worse.

One humid summer night around 9pm, I heard one of my sisters arguing with my mother in the basement. Thinking nothing of it, I continued to read my Dragon Ball Z comic book. My mother then came up to my room and asked, "Did you touch my daughter in any inappropriate way?" She was referring to my little sister who was about six years old at the time who lived with us. Claiming that someone had molested her while we were out at the park that day, I replied, "No, what are you talking about?" She then went over to my little sister and held a belt over her demanding that she tell her who touched her threatening that she would be whooped if she didn't give her a name. My little sister was with us throughout the whole day and we didn't see anyone touch her in the ways that our mother described. "This is just another of our mother's strange episodes." I said to myself in disappointment. As I heard my little sister faintly say, "No mommy, no one did anything to me!" I could not make out what was actually happening that night. It felt like none of what was going on was real. My mother then ran back downstairs to my sister and continued the argument. "Boom!" was the sound of the door after my sister stormed out of the front door in anger and frustration.

Coming up to the stairs to me, my mother walked into my room wearing clear plastic gloves and lifted my Nintendo 64 console off of the top of my TV. After examining the console to see if it could do enough damage to hit me in the head with, she placed it back atop the television and left my room. Still in fear, I sat frozen on my bed. Afraid to make any movement, I saw a rectangular shaped sharp shiny object with a hole in its left corner as my mother held it by its handle. As she walked quickly towards my room, I came to realize that the object that she was holding was in fact a meat cleaver.

Running to the front door before she reached my room, I ran down the street to my friend's house in fear and help. Banging on the door as endless tears rolled down my face, my friend finally opened the door. Breathing in terror, I yelled to her, "My mom is trying to murder us, call the police!" Once the police arrived, they inspected the house and found that she was unfit and on drugs after finding crack pipes throughout the house. With the police learning that we were living in the house for months with no electricity, gas, and water due to her drug use, they decided to ask us some questions. I recalled to them the times where it would be very cold in the house because there was not any heat and that we had to place washcloths in a bowl of water and put it in the microwave so that we can wash ourselves comfortably with a warm rag.

Although my sisters and I never knew what caused our mother to act strange and paranoid some nights, having clarity that she was on drugs helped us understand why she was acting the way she was. The police then asked me, "How would you feel if you were separated from your sisters?" I replied that it did not matter because I understood that we all needed to survive despite the condition that our mom was in and what she tried to do to us. Temporarily moving back to my grandmother's house in northeast Washington, D.C., my aunt gained full custody of my sisters and temporary custody of me hoping that my mother would get her life back together. We felt so bad that our little sister could not come with us to D.C. because we knew that it was unsafe for her to live with our mother. However, her father wanted to take care of her.

As my sisters and I longed for our mother's rehabilitation, it felt like it would never happen. That she would not be the mother who she is supposed to be because she never was. Trusting my aunt that our mother would get back on track, my sisters and I tried to move back to Maryland with our mother but she refused to let me in the house because she did not want me around my little sister. One of my oldest sisters decided to be homeless with me on the streets of Maryland because she knew that I did not do anything to our little sister and that she did not want me to face homelessness alone.

While living on the streets, we slept on our friends' couches and turned our shirts inside out because we did not have any clean clothes to wear. In the middle of the night, my sister would sneak in the basement of my mother's house to get a blanket for us to sleep under because my other sister would leave the patio door unlocked while we slept in a neighbor's car. Days later, we were able to get back in contact with our aunt and explained everything to her. My aunt then moved us back to live with her in Washington, D.C.

Chapter Three

Homelessness

To be back home living in the nation's capital was truly a blessing for me because things started to get better. As a 14 year old, I started to take life for what it was worth despite the bad things that I experienced in the past. Because my mother filed charges against me claiming that I molested my little sister, I caught myself standing in front of a judge in a family court in Maryland hoping that my future would not be ruined by my mother's crazy antics influenced by her drug use. At this point, I no longer viewed my mother as my mother because she ruined my life.

"Ross vs. Ross" the judge called as I stood on my feet to approach the stand. I looked to my right to find that my mother did not show up to the court. "This case is dismissed" said the judge as she banged her gavel. My sisters and I were happy of the decision after leaving the courtroom.

Getting back to trying to make a better life for myself, my aunt enrolled me into Browne Junior High School located in northeast Washington, D.C. and a summer camp with my cousin so that I would become more active as a teenager. However, I would say that growing up in the city was tough. It was very difficult for me to learn in school because it was filled with a lot of crime and bad students. This made me no longer interested in academics because of the negativity. I later attended the New School for Enterprise for Learning and Development Public Charter High School where I had to adjust to the rigors of high school. This school was cleaner and had less negativity and crime involved. The teachers were nice and really wanted us to succeed. Meanwhile, daily stress took over my aunt's character because she was responsible for a lot of things after my grandmother's death. With the stress from her job, taking care of my sisters and I along with her two children, and managing my grandmother's house after her death, it all began to take a toll on her ability to parent us.

One night, she received a call from my teacher about me not being on my best behavior. "Tired, tired, I'm just tired!" she yelled after hanging up the phone. "Anthony!" she yelled calling me down from my room. Stressed and angered, she walked in the kitchen and grabbed one of the heaviest frying pans that she could find from the bottom of the cabinet and chased me around the dining room table attempting to hit me with it. Out of the house I ran and down to my neighbor's.

Banging on my neighbor's door in fear once again in need of help brought back nostalgia from the night in Upper Marlboro in the summer of 2003 when I escaped my mother from murdering me. "What's going on?" the neighbors asked with a concerned look on their faces. I replied, "My aunt is trying to hit me with a frying pan; please call the police!" Upon the policeman's arrival and after my aunt calmed down, the police asked my aunt if there was anywhere else that I could live since she did not want to take care of me any longer. She replied, "Yes, he can go and live with my other sister located in southeast Washington, D.C."

I then moved to live with my other aunt who always believed that I was mistreated as a child and felt that no one was ever there to care for me. I shall say that this aunt always wanted to have fun when she visited my sisters and I when we lived with our grandmother. After leaving my aunt's house in northeast, I tried to return back to school the next day but the aunt whom I was living with would not allow me to go for some reason. My grandfather then put me in contact with my great uncle named Billy so that I can make some cash cutting grass to pay my aunt a reasonable amount of rent every month and put clothes on my back and shoes on my feet. Even though I was not in high school anymore and did not complete the ninth grade, I enjoyed staying with my aunt and my four younger cousins. However, after living with her for six months, she was not the "fun" aunt that she used to be. Aside from paying her rent and saving up enough cash to buy clothes and shoes for myself, she would ask me for money at times and I would give it to her without hesitation. It was not until I observed the alcoholic beverages packed on almost every rack of the refrigerator that I noticed that she was slowly becoming an alcoholic. Tired and sweaty coming back from a long day of work from cutting grass one night, she asked me for money once again. Calmly explaining to her that I was trying to save up enough cash to buy some new tennis shoes that I liked, she caught an attitude and began throwing my clothes out of her apartment and into the hallway of the living quarters.

Lying on my trash bags full of clothes, I hoped for a blanket to help shield me from the cold. It was close to 2am when the neighbors upstairs of the apartment building saw me sleeping on my trash bags filled with clothes. They invited me in to sleep comfortably for the night. The following morning, the tenant of the apartment went down stairs to ask my aunt if she could let me back in the apartment but it turned into an argument ending with my aunt throwing my birth certificate and social security card in my face as I sat on the staircase in hopes that she would let me back in. "You can have him!" are the words that she said before slamming her apartment door on her neighbor's face.

Thereafter, the tenant said that I could move in with her family. Attempting to report to work the next day to cut grass, my uncle Billy told me that I could no longer work for him because my aunt and grandfather told him to fire me. So there I was; homeless once again with no education and no job to take care of myself. The tenant was a 25 year old female who lived in a two bedroom one bathroom section 8 apartment with 13 other family members. I became an addition to the family by cooking for the kids and cleaning behind them. I made sure that I fulfilled my duties to the best of my ability because I knew that I needed a roof over my head.

While living with them, I experienced a whole different side of living in the streets. The father of the children was a hustler who sold drugs around the neighborhood because he believed that it was the only way that he could provide for his family. There were times where he would cut up crack on a plate with a razor blade while I sat next to him on a couch as if everything was normal. It was not normal to me because I was always told to stay away from drugs because I witnessed what it did to my mother and wanted no parts. I knew what he was doing was a bad thing but I had no choice but to deal with it because I knew the severity of me needing a place to lay my head. Other drug dealers in the neighborhood became envious of his drug sales and began to feud with him. Trying to protect his family, including me, we relocated to a three bedroom in section 8 housing in northeast to escape the hostility. As I helped them move their belongings, my aunt stood on the front porch of the apartment building watching me help them and never inviting me back to come live with her. This was deemed as one of the coldest moments in my life.

While living with the tenant and her family after relocating, some of the adults in the house believed that we should enroll into a program where we could earn a General Equivalency Diploma (G.E.D.) since none of us completed high school. My grandfather signed a notarized letter that allowed me into the program while the father of the children signed for me to obtain my first worker's permit. Working at Kentucky Fried Chicken marked my first commercial job held at age 16 as a food preparer. The general manager always motivated me to work hard because she was a very hard worker herself. Understanding that I needed to work to feed and clothe myself was my motivating factor to always do a good job.

After being enrolled in the G.E.D. program at the Perry School Community Service Center in northwest Washington, D.C., the family whom I was staying with advised that I go talk to one of the social workers at the school on a daily basis to keep my sanity because they knew that I had been through a lot prior to me living with them. However, I told them that they showed me the most love that I had ever felt from a family and that I didn't want the social worker to take me away from them. As months passed by, I took their advice and decided to see a social worker by the name of Carlton Brown. During our conversations, Mr. Brown would always tell me that he recognized potential in me and that he did not believe that the household that I was living in was a safe place for me because of the illegal activity that took place and the amount of people living in such little space.

One day, Mr. Brown offered that I come with him to check out an emergency homeless shelter called the Sasha Bruce House for homeless teenagers in northeast to see if it would be a better alternative for me. Upon arrival, the kids looked as if they were troubled. Mr. Brown then convinced me that I should give it a try. Trusting him, I sat down and filled out some paper work but after he left, I spent half of the day there because I believed that I did not belong so I trashed the paper work leaving the group home behind. Not telling the family members where I just came from, I returned to their home and continued living with them. While my sisters and aunt were not getting along too well in northeast, they soon departed ways. One of them went to start a new life in Virginia while the other lived with her aunt on her father's side of the family. Due to me not even knowing any members of my father's side, let alone the identity of my dad, I had no choice but to turn to the streets for housing.

About three months later, still in the G.E.D. program and working at KFC, I entered the house from a long day of work. Exhausted, I sat on the couch to rest my body. As I turned to the left cushion, I noticed some documents with my full name printed on them. I asked the grandmother who lived with us if she knew what the documents were about because they had my name on them. The grandmother was a very wise lady who I always sought knowledge from while I lived there. After asking out of curiosity, she informed me that the tenant who took me in was getting food stamps and welfare benefits in my name and that she did not want anyone to tell me. There were times when I could not get food from the refrigerator because the tenant had to feed her family but I was not aware that she was receiving income for me. After I asked the tenant if it was true, she caught an attitude and told me that she will stop using my name to get the benefits. I never asked her to stop the benefits because I knew that she needed them; I just wanted to know the truth and believed that it was my right to know although I was living in her house.

Later that night, some of her cousins were informed that I questioned her and decided to jump me and beat me up. The grandfather who lived with us was a construction worker who worked shifts starting as early as 5am. After I took the beating, I secretly asked him if he could wake me up at 5am so that I could pack my belongings and sit them in the backyard before everyone woke up the next morning. He said yes and I did just that.

That following morning, I returned to Mr. Brown's office telling him about what happened last night. He saw the knot on my head and asked me what happened. After explaining to him what happened, he replied, "I told you to get out of there when you had the chance. Let me see if I can find you somewhere to go." Diligently calling local shelters in the area, he found none with available spaces; even the one that I spent half the day in months before I was beat up. I was homeless yet again. Because I knew that it was after 5pm and raining outside, I knew that my social worker had a long day at work and wanted to go home. On his hard desk I laid while he tried to get in contact with my biological family members to see if there could be anywhere that I could go. My aunt in northeast told him that she tried to take care of me but she could not. He then called my grandfather; however, he claimed that there was no room for me where he was. My aunt then gave Mr. Brown my long lost uncle's number whom I did not see very often to see if he had a place. After a long conversation with the social worker, my uncle said yes that he would take me in. The next day, the family of 13 brought my belongings from their back yard where I left them to Mr. Brown's office.

Thereafter, I moved to Suitland, Maryland with my uncle who strongly believed that I should be re-molded into someone who he wanted me to become ignoring the fact that I was 16 years old and have already been exposed to surviving in the streets. Still in the G.E.D. program and working at KFC, the family members who enrolled in the program with me no longer attended. Six months after living with my uncle, he no longer wanted to take care of me anymore. In the middle of one night, he stood at the threshold of his front door holding the door wide open demanding me to leave. "Get out!" he yelled as I sat on the couch with tears rapidly rolling down my cheeks and onto my lap. Still sitting on the couch, he continued to yell, "Leave my damn house!" At this point, I began to realize that he was putting me out for no apparent reason and that he no longer wanted to deal with me. I gathered my thoughts, arose from the couch, and walked out of his apartment.

After he dropped me off at the subway station, in the cold I waited until the train began its route at 7am so that I could visit my job. When I first started working at KFC, I met a coworker by the name of Shakeena who was very concerned about my well-being ever since she learned of my undeserved past. She told me if I ever needed anything, to let her know. After arriving at my job, I told Shakeena that my uncle put me out. "You're lying" she replied after I told her the news. Minutes after conversing about what just happened, she said that I could come and live with her. I lived with Shakeena for about a week due to recurring arguments between her and her children's father in regards to me living there; I had no choice but to leave. Around 10pm on a Friday night, I sat in the back of a police car once again homeless with any place to go. I called Mr. Brown and explained to him why I could no longer live with Shakeena.

Tired of keep having to find a place to live, Mr. Brown told me to try the Sasha Bruce group home once again to see if there were any beds available. Taking his advice, I called the shelter. All of the beds were full except one. In a grateful and joyful tone, I told the administrator who picked up the phone that I was on my way. As I arrived, I stood on the porch knowing that this would be my only hope of survival and that I did not want to end up homeless again. I said to myself, "I have to get in here, see how they could help me, and make a better life for myself. I no longer have a family. My life can only get better from here."

Chapter Four

Starvation

So there I was. Living in an emergency homeless shelter filled with teenagers from all over the city. Some shy, some troubled, and some confused as to why they were here. The social workers here wanted to play an active role in our lives. After the first few counseling sessions, it took me some time getting used to them because it was very difficult to adapt to the transition. My train of thought was clouded and disabled me to think clearly. Different teens would sleep in the shelter throughout the night due to how quickly some of them came and left. For the first few nights, I slept with one eye open and made sure that all of my belongings were protected. We all would gather in the morning for breakfast and dinner to share with the social workers on how our days at school were. This was also a time for us to bond with one another because we all came from different walks of life. Some of them were placed in the shelter to be taught a lesson by their parents because they acted out at home too much and their parents wanted them to realize that other's had it worse than them.

Getting closer to earning my G.E.D., I left KFC and began working part-time as a barista and cashier at Starbucks in northwest D.C. This was an upgrade from KFC because the pay rate was better and it marked my first job where I qualified for benefits and tips. I also began working as a food runner and host at Ruby Tuesday in Arlington, Virginia at Pentagon City Mall. This was a more mature environment because the majority of waiters and waitresses were parents or in college earning tips to make a living and pay for their education. I wanted to be a waiter but had to be 18 or older and I was 16 years old at the time. It was not until after I turned 18 that I began waiting tables and earning tips. I would wake up in the morning, take a shower, attend the G.E.D. program, work at Starbucks during the day, Ruby Tuesday during the night, go back to the group home, and start all over again the next day. It was my lifestyle. After six months of attending G.E.D. classes, I was eligible to take the practice exam and then the final exam afterwards.

Months after learning, studying, and practicing, I was excited that I had passed the practice exam. Now all I needed to do was to knock out the final exam to earn the equivalent of a high school diploma despite not being able to finish high school because of my journey of homelessness. Months later as I scheduled to take the final exam, I was turned away because I was not 18 or over, legally emancipated from my mother, or had a parent or guardian to sign for me. I had no choice but to wait until I turned 18 to be eligible. During the hiatus, I decided to continue stacking my money from working both jobs and work on learning how to drive so that I could earn my drivers license until I was eligible to take the final G.E.D. examination. I later relocated to another group home in the city owned by Sasha Bruce Youthwork.

This group home came equipped with more services such as a life skills program, weekly allowance, exercise training, and all other programs needed to prepare us to live independently to help achieve stability. I remember when the director of the group home, Daryl Sanders, would take me for driving lessons at a local park on the weekend. "Take your time and focus." said Mr. Sanders as I would slowly press my foot against the gas pedal because he made sure that I took care of his vehicle while I was learning. It was times like this that made me realize that the social workers really cared for us and that they wanted us to succeed. I obtained my learners permit at age 15 and my provisional drivers license at age 16 and my adult license after I turned 18.

Returning back to the G.E.D. program where I attended classes, I brushed up for six months because I was now of age to take the exam. After the refresher, I went to take the exam. Looking forward at a chalkboard in front of me, I listened to the proctor read the instructions of the exam aloud. "You have four and a half hours to complete the exam. There will be a 15 minute break after each section. You may begin!" As the test started to come to a close, I pressed the dull point of my no. 2 pencil on the answer sheet to bubble in my last question. I breathed in and out as the feeling of completing the test made me feel a whole lot better inside. As weeks passed, I waited anxiously to receive my score. Darkness began to cloud my eyesight as the administrator informed me that I failed the test.

Days after sulking in defeat, I went back to the program to brush up for another six months in addition to having a couple of personal tutors come to the shelter and tutor me religiously. One of my tutors, Dr. Edwards, would always ride his bicycle to the group home on bright early mornings throughout the weekday to tutor me in geometry, algebra, and trigonometry. I always asked him how I could repay him and he always told me to keep aspiring to gain more knowledge and continue to seek higher education. I could tell that he had a passion for teaching and felt good about himself when his work paid off. Six months later after preparing for the exam again, I was ready to take the exam again. This time, it felt like more of a breeze and I was confident enough that I had performed well. After hearing that my score improved a couple of hundred points, I jumped into the air yelling, "I just passed my G.E.D! Yeah!!!" in excitement. Everyone in the group home congratulated me and was excited themselves. The following week, I ran down to a College Bound program located in the basement of the Perry School. Huffing and puffing I ran to Ms. Ebony Lea, the director of the program, and told her that I just earned my G.E.D. and wanted to go to college. The employees at College Bound always touched base with me while I was in the G.E.D. program to make sure that I was doing well.

Trying to calm the excitement, Ms. Ebony told me to breathe and take a seat. She then grabbed a thick paperback book the size of a phone book and sat it on my lap. The book was filled with different colleges and universities across the country. As I flipped through the pages, she asked, "Do you know what school you want to go to? If so, look at the schools' requirements to see if you meet them." (meaning that I had to look for schools that accepted my G.E.D. because not all colleges and universities did at the time). The very first school that I saw was Harvard University located in Cambridge, Massachusetts. Knowing that this was one of the top schools in the world, I wanted to apply there but the school did not accept people with G.E.D.'s.

I then flipped to colleges and universities in the North Carolina section. This is where a small accredited private four-year institution piqued my interest. They accepted people with high school diplomas and G.E.D.'s. African Americans made up 95% of the population and it was a notable historically black college in the south. "This is the school that I want to attend!" I yelled to Ms. Ebony. "What's the name?" she asked with a smile on her face. "Saint Augustine's College!" I said in exuberance. (The school later changed its name to Saint Augustine's University in 2012.) I chose this school because it was a small four year college that could have potentially help me learn some things that I may have missed from not attending high school because of its small class sizes. I wanted to start off small and not stumble into a big university and flunk out. Because Ms. Ebony knew some students who had attended the school, she felt confident that I could attend and suggested that I attend a summer bridge program held at Gallaudet University.

Although she recommended that I attend the program, I was not so accepting because I felt that I would feel like an outsider and that students from my generation would not be accepting of me due to my background. All I could remember was sitting in G.E.D. classes with 40 and 50 year old people. I could not imagine being back within my age group. For this reason, I told Ms. Ebony no and that I would think about it. After leaving her office, her coworker handed me a pack of flashcards filled with vocabulary words to help me prepare for the SAT's/ACT's.

"O-V-E-R-Z-E-A-L-O-U-S" was one of many of the vocabulary words that I spelled aloud while pacing back and forth in the group home. After a week-long of studying and enhancing my vocabulary, I changed my mind and told Ms. Ebony that I would accept her offer to attend the summer bridge program. Who knew that this decision would change my life forever? The program was filled with students from all over the city who were about to embark on their collegiate careers. I took this opportunity to surround myself around the smartest group of students that I could find. I always listened and observed as I watched intelligent minds work together. After leaving my comfort zone, I became friends with this guy named William. Will was always quick to answer questions asked in regards to algebra and geometry. It was just what I needed; to learn from someone who excelled in math so that I could earn the SAT/ACT score needed to gain admission to Saint Augustine's College. After attending the program for a couple of days, I asked Will if we could meet up at a library to see how he could help me to get better at algebra and geometry. After agreeing that we will meet, he never showed up to the library a couple times. I thought that I would never learn the skills needed until one day he finally showed up.

Will spoke for hours about the material and handed me a DVD collection set filled with geometry videos to watch. I would go home, pop them in the DVD player, and watch them while I paused and rewound the content to take notes for review.

While attending the program, Ms. Ebony introduced me to a lady named Jaime Willis. Jaime served as the Chief Financial Officer (CFO) for a non-profit organization called LevelTen. LevelTen sought to close the achievement gap in America by collaborating with many educational enrichment programs around the country to reach its goal. When Jaime first caught wind to my story from Ms. Ebony, she decided that she would try to help me make it to college. Jaime scheduled a time for us to meet at a local library near my group home. While there, we discussed the financial aid portion of college and how I could receive more funding. However, during the conversation, tears started to roll down Jaime's face as I told her that I was running out of time and that I was not going to see the day that I would attend college. As tears continued to roll down her face, people in the library looked on as she replied, "You are going to make it. You're not running out of time." This is where I felt that her dedication was real because she cared so much about my future and believed in me. Before we left the library, Jaime wrote down an address and asked that I meet her later that night on U. Street. She said that she wanted to introduce me to someone who she thought could help me as well.

From street to street, I looked anxiously in excitement because I did not know who this mysterious important person whom Jaime wanted me to meet. As I arrived at the doorstep of an upscale restaurant, I looked up at the tall building to see if the address matched the same that Jaime had written down earlier on a sticky note. As I walked in, it was like I stepped into a place that I did not belong. There were people wearing nice professional attire discussing business over wine and hors d'oeuvres. It seemed as if I was amongst the rich making business deals with one another.

Navigating my way through the guests, Jaime directed me to where the man was whom she wanted me to meet. There he stood; in the back of the room, low-key away from the general crowd. As soon as I walked up to him, he introduced himself to be Paul Brunson. The Chief Executive Officer (CEO) of the non-profit organization LevelTen who had international relations with Bächëshir Ügur Educational Institutions in Istanbul, Turkey. "Jaime told me a lot about you." said Paul as I shook his hand. He then introduced me to a nearby college student by the name of Regis DeVeaux.

Regis was a Morehouse student who was deeply in love with Christianity. While speaking to Regis, I explained to him that I looked up to people like him and that I wanted to be in the "circle" that he was a part of. The "circle" meaning that I wanted to be surrounded by nothing but positive and successful people. I also told him that I was running out of time and wish that I could be in his shoes of being a college student. Regis replied, "You're not running out of time. You're only 18 years old. You'll make it."

"You have done well for yourself." said Paul. "If there was one thing that I could give to you, what would it be? It could be a car; anything. What would it be?" Paul said as he took a sip of his wine. I turned to look at him and replied, "Anything?" as my eyes bulged out of my face. I then looked up to the ceiling thinking about all of the possible things that I could ask for. I replied in question, "A Lamborghini?!" Paul replied, "Anything." I looked up to the ceiling once more and took a look at all of the business people that I was surrounded by. I then said to him, "Take me under your wing." Paul replied, "Done!" Who knew that out of all of the possible things that I could have asked for, this would be the most fruitful that would forever change my life? "Here's an address that I want you to meet me at. Be there 10am sharp." he said

35

as he handed me a napkin with an address belonging to the location of his office in Arlington, Virginia.

The next morning, I arrived at his office situated in a tall white building. As soon as I walked in, Paul handed me $100. I instantly gave it back and told him that I didn't take money from anyone; especially if I didn't earn it. He said that he wanted me to get my first pair of slacks, a white dress shirt, and a tie with the $100 bill. He also called me his new intern. This marked my first internship ever as I became the assistant to the CEO of LevelTen.

On my first day, I proved how much resiliency I had by working a whopping 19 hour shift. From morning to night, Paul and I spent the entire day together getting to know one another while waiting on his Turkish friend, Gokan, [pronounced; (Go-Kahn)] from a delayed flight. Tired we were in the airport, but the time was well spent. The reason why I asked Paul to take me under his wing was because I wanted to reach the level of success that he accomplished. He was a very influential person and was well connected. He also worked with foreign exchange students from Turkey through an organization called Inlingua. Just seeing so many Turkish students and how they interacted with the American lifestyle was refreshing because I never experienced something like it before. This also marked my first time tasting Turkish delight and baklava. Although I can recall the baklava to taste better than the Turkish delight, they both brought an indescribable sweet taste to my tongue because I never tried them before.

Weeks after working for Paul, he started to become a father figure in my eyes because our relationship went beyond the internship. We attended gym together to work out and built a true rapport that a mentor and mentee should always have. It was simply a dream come true because I still didn't know who my dad was or what he looked like. Transitioning from working at Starbucks and Ruby Tuesday, I became a cashier at a sandwich shop called Potbelly, in uptown D.C. As I continued to prepare for the SAT/ ACT's, not only were tutors coming out to the shelter to tutor me, but I also stayed up until 3am and 4am watching tutorial videos on YouTube via Yaymath.org. Yaymath was a website where the instructor, Robert Ahdoot, would hold live tutorials with students learning different areas of math. Whether it was algebra, trigonometry, the quadratic formula, functions, or logarithms, I learned them all from Mr. Ahdoot's teachings. Out of all of the YouTube tutorials that I watched to prepare for the math portion of the ACT's, I learned the easiest from Yaymath.

This is where I began to starve. This is where I became hungry; hungry for education. Ambitious and motivated to go out in the world and make a better life for myself. I was eager to learn because I wasn't living for anything else at the time. I knew that I did not want to end up dead or in jail because I was simply not about that lifestyle. I wanted to make a better life for myself. I could have been dead a long time ago but I wasn't. God provided me with a shelter to live in that provided stable living. Many of the youth in the group home did not take advantage of the services that the shelter provided; however, I took full advantage because it was all I had. I was motivated by many successful people in the world. They were the ones who kept me going.

There was also a very bright girl in the shelter who held a 3.7 GPA in high school. She had both of her parents but they put her in there so that she could get her act together. She received praise by all of the social workers due to the intelligence that she exhibited. She was also college bound on her way to Florida Agricultural and Mechanical University (FAMU). Every chance I got, I sat down with her to prepare for the ACT's because she scored very well on a similar exam, the SAT's. It was as if I became a leech sucking and absorbing all of the knowledge from her needed to score well.

One of the social workers in the shelter, Mr. George Montgomery, drove me down to Raleigh, North Carolina to tour Saint Augustine's University so that I could see if it was really something that I could adapt to and explore my potential. As soon as we stepped foot on campus, it was as if I had stepped into a dream. I began to touch the walls that were made out of stone because it felt so surreal. Mr. Mangum from the admissions office acted as our tour guide who provided a lot of information of the different buildings and departments. After the tour was over, he asked me to recall the name of each building as a quiz. Luckily, I was able to recite the name of each building learned in excitement. After the tour was over, Mr. George and I were on our way back to D.C. The visit at the school felt like I stepped into my dream and walked out of it.

Before President Obama won his first election in 2008, I scheduled to take the ACT's at Eastern Senior High School. I could not sleep an inch the night before the exam because I knew that the results would be part of the determining factor of me attending college. With my mind racing all night, I was able to wake up and achieve a score required to be admitted on conditions at the university. Moving along the other parts of the application, I needed to have enough money to make sure that I could attend the institution. I searched Google for scholarships for minorities and homeless youth. Throughout my findings, I clicked on a link of an organization called the National Association for the Education of Homeless Children and Youth. NAEHCY provided scholarships and services for students who experienced homelessness and had faced child neglect while growing up whom wished to seek higher education. I contacted the Policy Director, Ms. Barbara Duffield, and told her my story. Ms. Duffield was able to process my application almost a year early to be considered for the LeTendre (pronounced; [la-tawn]) Scholars class of 2009. Ms. Duffield was very concerned about my situation and wanted to help me the best way possible.

After marching to the polls to vote for then presidential candidate, Barack Obama, Mr. Mangum from the admissions office at Saint Augustine's University called me on the phone. I spoke to him for about an hour on the reasons why I should be admitted into the school. I explained to him that I wanted to make a better life for myself and that I didn't want to remain in a shelter for the rest of my life. After explaining to him that I was motivated by then presidential candidate Barack Obama's willpower and courage to run for President of the United States as an African American, I told him that I wouldn't want anything more but to strive for greatness. Thereafter, Mr. Mangum said two words to me that I will never forget that changed my life: "You're in!" he said as I held my right ear tightly to my T-Mobile flip-phone. I was so excited that I could not even believe what just happened. A long pause took place realizing that I had just been accepted into college.

Chapter Five

Living the Dream, Earning the Victory, and Harvard Law School

After the news of me getting accepted into college spread throughout the group home and local shelters in D.C., I had to prepare for the future. The excitement grew even more when staff members of Sasha Bruce Youthwork constructed a care package for me before I started my journey. Ink pens, tablets, three-ring binders, pocket folders, pencils, and other school supplies were packed in a book bag made especially for me. North Carolina bound I was as I waited anxiously for Paul's arrival to transport me four hours down south from the shelter. I left the group home with over $5,000 saved from the jobs I worked and a large stack of papers with notes full of the advanced math that I learned from YouTube.

Hours into the drive down south, I started to notice a change in the climate and culture. The rims on the cars were the size of a five year old baby. "Boom!, Thud!, Boom!" was all I heard from sub-woofers in the trunks of the cars while the drivers smiled to show their shiny gold grills as we stopped at the stop lights. "I guess this is the southern hospitality and lifestyle that everyone was warning me about." I chuckled to myself. Once I arrived on campus, I could not believe it. I could not believe that I was about to officially begin to live my dream to make a better life for myself despite my undeserving past. After Paul helped me move in, we took a walk outside and he looked around the campus. He then turned to me and said these last words that I would never forget: "You know what Ant, you could easily become the king of this thing." (meaning that I could conquer the collegiate atmosphere and become a great leader to my society).

I started to get used to the southern lifestyle weeks after my first semester had begun. Different from Washington, D.C., the south was more spacious and slower. The people were friendlier and the cost of living was much cheaper. I knew that I was taking a risk before I left the group home because it provided a stable roof over my head. However, I did not want to remain in the shelter because although I ended up homeless at such a young age, I still had a chance to explore my potential. I did not want to waste what others saw in me. They really believed in me and I did not want to let them down.

After adjusting to the campus, I believed that I was in the right place because the school was a small private college with an enrollment of about 1,500 to 2,000 students that were predominately African American which helped me feel more connected. The college's track team also had a notable long-standing national outdoor track and field record for division two. I had confidence that I could capitalize and graduate with a proficient grade point average because of the potential that everyone saw in me.

Living the Dream

During my first semester, I was so stringent upon studying because people told me different myths about college. Some said that if I did not perform well academically, I would be kicked out and end up homeless again while others claimed that I would be kicked out for financial reasons. Because I was naive, I tried to avoid the worse from happening. I stayed away from the in-crowd and the students that always wanted to party. I was incognito from the student body, anti-social, and joined no clubs or organizations. I also sat in the front row of the classroom and took as much notes as possible to make sure that I didn't miss anything. Spending four to six hours a day in the library, I was able to study ahead of the syllabi and earn a 4.0 grade point average my first semester. Because I had never earned a 4.0 GPA before because I did not go to high school, this meant so much to me and was a huge accomplishment coming from a G.E.D. program.

Towards the end of the semester, I called the director of the shelter that I left in D.C. to let her know that I would need a place to live while the campus closed down for the summertime. The director was understanding and saved a bed for my return. After returning back to the group home, I noticed that the same homeless youth that were there when I lived there were no longer there but replaced by other homeless youth. As I spoke to them, I explained that I slept in the same bed that they were sleeping in before I went off to college and that they could do anything that they put their minds to. I also noticed that my SAT and ACT preparation books were still on the shelf where I left them before I went off to school. After sharing my story with them, there was a young boy who just graduated from high school and wanted to go to college. He said that he looked up to me and that he wanted to seek higher learning. I then sat him down in the same chair that I sat in when my tutors tutored me and fed him the same advice that my mentors and supporters had given me. I explained to him that he was going to make it and that I sat in the same chair that he was sitting in with someone in my seat telling me that I was going to make it. After assisting him with SAT preparation during my stay, he later got accepted into a community college in Prince George's County Maryland.

Before the start of the summer, I was invited to serve as a guest speaker at the British Embassy. To know that tickets were about $750 to attend the event that night and that I was the keynote speaker blew my mind. The British Embassy was adorned with expensive yellow colored drapes and had columns made of marble stone situated around each corner. The stairs were beautiful with red velvet carpet running down them. It was simply amazing. Rubbing shoulders with people such as Congresswoman and delegate Eleanor Holmes Norton, former Speaker of the House Nancy Pelosi, and many other prominent politicians felt as if I was living another dream. The five-star dinner was delicious and the people were very friendly.

Minutes before my speech, I walked to the restroom. Washing his hands was someone who looked familiar. It wasn't until he turned around that I noticed that it was the Mayor of D.C. himself, Adrian Fenty. Not saying anything to him, I walked to the stall. After using the restroom, it was my turn to speak. Speaking to the crowd implementing the oratorical skills learned throughout prior interviews, I was able to catch the embassy's full attention. After I spoke about overcoming adversity as a homeless youth to earning a 4.0 GPA freshmen year, people from the audience came up to shake my hand and took several photos with me including Mayor Fenty and his assistant. As he shook my hand, he told me that he wanted me to come and work in his office. I replied in awe and excitement, "Are you serious or is this just for the cameras?" "I'm serious" he said with a smile on his face. "Give my assistant your email and look out for something in your inbox tomorrow morning."

From that moment on, my life changed. This is where I began to live my dream. The dream of being a college student and soaring for nothing but greatness. When I returned home that night, I was elated and could not sleep. My mind was racing knowing that I was about to work for the Mayor of the nation's capital. It was truly a dream come true. Eager to check my inbox the next morning, the content of the email sent from his assistant entailed that I send my résumé and come into the office so that they could get me started as soon as possible.

On that following Monday, I caught the subway downtown to the city hall. After placing my belongings on the belt through the metal detectors, I was searched meticulously by the security guards. Nice ties and business suits were worn in sophistication by members of his administration. "Welcome to the Bullpen." said the Chief of Staff as she politely greeted me at the tall glass doors of his office. The office was called the bullpen because it was the brain behind his work. While working there, I was introduced to a guy who always wore trendy bow ties and a nice suit. One day, his continued sense of fashion caught my attention prompting me to ask him, "How do you tie your bow ties? They look nice and I would sure love to go back to school in the fall with a sense of style." He answered, "I learned from watching videos on YouTube. It took me over 100 tries but you'll get the hang of it." After waking up in the mornings watching different videos on how to tie a bow tie, I failed miserably. However, after several retries, I finally got the hang of it with the assistance from a police officer who patrolled the Mayor's office daily. I would also see the Mayor and President Obama wear matching ties together for press conferences and perform collaborative initiatives first-hand.

The internship not only marked the first time that I learned how to tie a bow tie, but it also was the first to expose me to the application of politics and helped enhance my professionalism in the workplace. Working in the Office of

Legislative Affairs, Department of Employment Services (DOES), the District Attorney's office, and the Department of Communications where they prepared speeches for the Mayor, all served a valuable purpose.

Before I returned back to school in the fall, I was invited to attend a Student Leadership retreat by the President of my university. The retreat allowed me to spend a week in the cabins with other student leaders from the campus to brainstorm ideas on how to get the student body more socially involved for the upcoming academic year. I would say that this is where I was "raw." I state the word raw because I had the mentality of not allowing anyone to get in the way of my success and that no one could do what I did; which was to come from being a homeless teen to earning a 4.0 GPA my first semester in college after earning a G.E.D. However, others helped me realize that the mentality that I had was absolutely not the mindset to have because I wasn't the only person in the world who had a story.

Weeks into the start of my second semester, I noticed an email from the National Association for the Education of Homeless Children and Youth (NAEHCY) sitting in my inbox. The email was an invitation to attend a scholarship banquet with 14 other students who faced homelessness and was neglected as a child. The purpose of the conference was to fly us out to Denver, Colorado so that we could share our stories with one another and build the bond of a family that we never had. Because I had never flown before, I did not know what to expect as I sat in the backseat of the taxi on my way to the airport. Nervously I sat with my back against the taxi's leather seats as I waited to embark on my mini adventure. This was very new to me because I have never been to Denver, Colorado; however, those who have been informed me of the climate and to bring warm clothing because of the cold weather. They also told me to make sure that I was at the airport at least two hours early because of the process I would have to undergo by the Transportation Security Administration (TSA) that could take several minutes.

While waiting in the terminal of the airport, I spoke to my mentors about my skepticism of flying. They told me not to worry, relax, and chew bubble gum to control my ears from popping due to the altitude of the flight. Upon boarding the plane, I placed my carry-on bag in the compartment above my seat and sat by the window. As I placed my seatbelt around me properly, I listened carefully to the flight attendant's safety instructions. Up, up, and away I went as the plane took off in full throttle as I prayed for the safety of others and myself. Despite the turbulence, it was smooth sailing minutes after takeoff. "Snap!" sounded my camera as I took pictures of the clouds from my window seat as the plane glided through the clouded blue sky effortlessly. I placed my earphones in my ear and pressed play on my iPod to listen to some hip hop as I laid back in relaxation and closed my eyes. "Yes! I survived the plane ride" I said to myself as the wheels of the plane hit the ground of its destination.

Walking to the gate where representatives of NAEHCY were said to meet us, I saw members of the organization holding a big sign that read, "LeTendre Scholar's Over Here!" I then met up with the other scholars who flew in around the same time as I. We all introduced ourselves and where we were from. After checking in at the hotel and getting settled, we shared our backgrounds and why we attended the trip. Although only 15 of us were chosen, there were students there from all over the country. Some of them were from California, New York, Idaho, Georgia, Connecticut, Texas, Oregon, Florida, and so forth with me being the only person from Washington, D.C. I have never visited any of the states mentioned which made this a good opportunity to learn all about them.

While sharing our stories with one another, we all realized that some had it worse than others and experienced similar events. Adapting to the cold weather in the city, we spent about a week in Denver getting to know one another. Wined and dined we were as the chaperones took us to eat at restaurants such as the Cheesecake Factory and other eateries. We also attended a hockey game which marked my first time attending the sporting event and being introduced to the fundamentals of the game. It was very cold during the game but just to see all of the other students having a good time and enjoying themselves made me feel good inside.

Later in the week we attended the scholarship banquet to share our stories to over 700 policy-makers representing all 50 states of America. This was the biggest crowd that I had ever spoken in front of in my life. However, the students and I were able to deliver our messages well in which we received a standing ovation from the crowd. After spending a few days in Denver, me having the time of my life was about to come to a close. Before saying our farewells, we exchanged numbers and added each other on Facebook to keep in touch. As I rode the cab back to the airport, I was thinking that we may not see one another again due to how everyone lived in different places. However, some of us were optimistic that we would meet again someday.

Back down south I landed to continue my semester. This year, I wanted to take an approach different from my first semester where I spent majority of my time in the library studying. I wanted to branch out more and find myself. I began getting involved in organizations such as the pre-law society where I served as the secretary of the club to prepare students for their future of attending law school. I knew that I wanted to someday go to law school so I got involved as much as I could to learn more of what it entailed. One night as I was walking to my room after taking a long day of classes, the Dean of Students reported that there will be an event at North Carolina State University sponsored by a local academy named after Dr. Cornel West. Dr. West was a political figure who graduated from Harvard and Princeton University. He was a philosopher, professor, activists, author, and prominent member of the Democratic Socialists of America.

Because everyone was talking about the event, I hopped on the shuttle bus going to NC State with the other students. As we arrived, the line was very long to get in the doors because the event was well promoted throughout the state and piqued a lot of people's interest. As I asked questions about the event, I learned that the Cornel West Academy of Excellence focused on the lives of at-risk youth in grades 2nd through 6th to help build their literacy, self-esteem, and critical thinking skills. Finally able to sit down, I noticed about 40 to 50 young boys dressed in black polo shirts and khaki pants on the stage introducing themselves as prominent African American leaders such as Dr. Martin Luther King Jr., Marcus Garvey, Malcolm X, Ralph Bunche, and other civil rights activists. At the event, a young boy that looked as if he was in the 2nd grade stood on a chair adjusting the microphone to his level to deliver the introduction for Dr. West. I sat in awe as the little boy delivered the introduction eloquently with confidence and precision. It was absolutely jaw-dropping.

After the event was over, I felt the need to get involved in the organization someway, somehow due to the riveting effect of the students' performance. Because there were so many people vying to take pictures with the boys and Dr. West, I could not reach the President of the academy to share my thoughts and willingness to become involved. However, I was able to reach the Vice President, Mr. Deron Medley. I went to him and asked if I could volunteer because I saw so much potential in the program and the little boys and wanted to be there for them hoping my story would help them become great leaders in the world. Mr. Deron recorded my number in his phone and told me that he would contact me tomorrow morning. While riding the shuttle bus back to campus, I felt good inside knowing that I was about to put some of my free time to use to potentially change someone else's for the better.

About 9am on Saturday morning, Mr. Deron sent me a text message asking to meet him at the front of my campus' entrance in an hour. Quickly jumping out of my bed, I took a shower and got dressed to meet him. During the ride to the Marbles Kids Museum, we became acquainted with one another before we met up with the others from the academy. As we arrived, I saw the members of the academy in a group wearing black tee shirts and khaki pants. I stepped out of the car to meet the boys and later was introduced to Mr. Deron's brother and President of the academy, Antoine Medley. Mr. Antoine was a graduate of Virginia Tech and was very concerned about the well-being and future of at-risk youth which motivated him to start the academy. Working diligently throughout the day with the boys, I wanted to become a permanent mentor. Since volunteering, I was able to help with curriculum planning and activities for the academy as well as become a mentor to the kids.

As the semester began to wrap up, I not only became more involved on campus and in the community, but I also interacted more with the student body by becoming the

Executive Assistant to the President of the Student Government Association.

"Uh, oh; it's that time again" I said to myself as a reminder that I would need to find a place to live once again due to the campus closing down for the holidays. Although this was one of the major obstacles that I thought about before leaving the group home, I never had to live in the shelter again because of all of the help that I was surrounded by. I was able to meet new people on campus who invited me to spend Thanksgivings and Christmases with their families due to me never being assigned a foster care family and having no contact with any of my family members since I was in the shelter.

During one Thanksgiving and Christmas break, I lived with a friend named Chris Anderton and his family. Chris was a senior and a close friend whom I had met my second semester that was a member of a fraternity and was always in the gym working out. Although he allowed me to live with his family for free, I still wanted to contribute something to the household. For this reason, I asked close friend and supporter, Ms. Duffield if she could donate some food for me for the holidays. Ms. Duffield wanted to play a pivotal role in my life because she cared about me a whole lot. She would always remind me of the time when I first called her to apply for a scholarship from NAEHCY during President Obama's election season. After I explained to her that I would be living with a friend during the break, she offered to donate $400 so that I would be financially secure. I thanked her and told her that I would be able to pay her back someday.

Still keeping in touch with Paul, whom later began to work for Oprah Winfrey becoming a Modern Day Matchmaker, I shared with him all of my accomplishments from my first year. Days before Christmas day, Paul sent me a text message telling me that he wanted to sign the title of his 1994 Nissan Pathfinder truck over to me. I could not believe it because while I was in D.C., there were times where Paul would always drive around in the truck and I would say to him, "Paul, you have all of this money but still drive this? Why don't you get a Lamborghini or something? You do know that you don't have to drive this right? Or, you can just give it to me?" I said prayerfully hoping that he would give in. Paul replied, "See, Ant, that's how a lot of people go broke. You don't need to spend a lot of money on expensive things when you can find something cheaper that gets the job done." So, I decided to stop pressing him to buy another car and continued wishing that he would take my advice and give it up to me. And yes, that day came. The truck only had 80,000 miles on it and was barely driven. Although this was the longest 20 days that I had waited in my life to get behind the wheel of my first car, I couldn't sleep and constantly daydreamed about swerving around the corner of my dormitory on campus when school started back up. The countdown was simply a nightmare because I could not stop thinking about it. During the wait, Chris had just gotten his car from his uncle and wanted to teach me how to drive. Even though I was taught years ago back in D.C., I needed to brush up.

After sharpening my driving skills, I met up with Paul in D.C. to obtain the vehicle. Later that night, Paul wanted to see how well I could drive by riding with me around the city. "You sure you can drive like that?" Paul asked as he looked down at my feet to see that I was wearing Nike flip flops as I started to press my foot on the pedal. I replied, "I got this." As I pressed my foot gently on the break to switch the gears before pulling off. A few minutes into the drive, "You're about to kill me!" Paul yelled as we found ourselves in the middle of the street with cars passing by on both sides. After getting us out of the middle of the road, he told me to slow down and started asking me to read the street names aloud to him as we started to approach them because he suspected that something was wrong with my vision. Noticing that I could not read the names aloud to him, he told me that I needed eyeglasses because I could not see well from afar. He explained to me that I would need to obtain eyeglasses before he could sign the truck over to me because I could potentially get into a car accident. I knew that I had bad eyesight when I sat far away from the chalkboard in class because words would become jumbled and blurred causing me to always sit in the front of the class. Taking Paul's advice into consideration, I had no choice but to buy eyeglasses because I really wanted to drive the car back down to Raleigh when school started back again.

The next morning, I called around to shops such as LensCrafters and Hour Eyes looking to find the best price for eyeglasses. Throughout the day, I visited different stores to find the right fit. Some optometrists recommended that I try wearing contacts because the frames for eyeglasses were quite expensive. Taking their advice, I sat in the store for an hour in a half trying to fit the contacts in my eye but my top eyelid kept closing down every time it felt the lens getting closer to my eyeball. Minutes after battling with my top eyelid, I gave up and settled for eyeglasses. The next day, Paul and I headed to the Department of Motor Vehicles (DMV) to switch over the title. I asked him, "So how much money do I need to give you for the truck? He replied, "$1" with a smile on his face.

He then handed me the keys after we submitted the paperwork to the lady at the front desk.

North Carolina bound I was again. This time, it was me driving myself down instead of someone else. I could finally put the drivers license that I earned before I went off to college to use. Driving down to Raleigh I was after I took a nap so that I could stay awake for the four hour drive that I had ahead of me. While driving on the highway, the reality of me driving became surreal. Adjusting to the truck felt very easy for me as I maintained the speed limit and drove carefully. Although it was an older vehicle, students looked at me as I arrived on campus congratulating me on my new ride. I felt like the man because some students didn't have vehicles in college and I was blessed to have one at the time.

After being heavily involved in my campus community, I was appointed to be the Executive Secretary of the SGA by then Student Body President, Masac Dorlouis. Masac (pronounced; [may-zack]) was a Florida native with a Haitian background and ancestry. He too was heavily involved as a student leader and knew that he would someday run for President of the Student Government. It was like we were Batman and Robin. Whenever he ran late for meetings, he would call me and I would be there to fill in until his arrival.

"Clutch" was the word that he would call me whenever I came through during dire times. And since then, we have been able to help each other grow as leaders and positive role models in today's society.

Back in 2009 when I spoke at the scholarship conference in Denver, a white couple approached me from the crowd because they were very impressed about my story and wanted to support me. They informed me that they had an extra room at their home in Greensboro and that they wanted me to come live with them. Knowing that I would need a place to live when the campus closed down, I told them that I would contact them if I needed the room. As the summer of 2010 approached, I wanted to take the couple up on their offer and spend the summer with them. The family was an older couple in their early 50's that owned a nice home and earned good income. The husband was a police officer and the wife worked for the state in regards to higher education. After getting settled in, I applied for a couple jobs at restaurants because I had prior history of being a waiter. After getting hired at Olive Garden full-time and being rehired part-time at Ruby Tuesday, I was able to support myself financially at the moment.

After a couple of weeks of living with them, I started to notice a sudden change in their behavior. It was as if they weren't as happy as they were when I first met them. After coming in the house from a long night of waiting tables from a double shift on a Friday night, the husband told me to come join him at the table. Looking depressed, he informed me that his wife was no longer happy and that I needed to pack my belongings and leave the house before Sunday no later than 6:30pm.

Puzzled, I asked him if I did anything wrong. He replied, "There were times when you didn't make your bed and we became really annoyed by that." I replied softly, "But no one ever brought it to my attention so how was I supposed to know that it was bothering you guys?" He replied, "No one should have had to tell you." After the conversation, I politely excused myself from the table and walked upstairs to my room feeling bad inside knowing that I just got put out for not making my bed. To me, this seemed like a lame excuse to be the cause of their unhappiness. However, I remembered that weeks ago when I informed the wife that I was tired of being abused and used and did not want to go through similar treatment again, her behavior started to change weeks later. I guess that they had plans of trying to use me for something and by me kindly letting them know up front unbeknownst, it ruined their plans and I no longer became any use to them anymore.

Calling listings on Craigslist for vacant rooms, I had no luck. It was the weekend and a lot of places that could help me find housing did not open back up until Monday. For this reason, I asked the family if they could extend the timeframe for me to leave, however, they said, "No." Hours later, I received a call back from a lady named Yvonne whom I found through a listing on Craigslist that had a vacant room. Unfortunately, she informed me that someone had already snagged the room as I arrived at her doorstep. There I was; homeless yet again in the middle of Greensboro.

Later that day, Ms. Yvonne remembered that a close friend of hers by the name of Audrey Harris had a basement that I could potentially rent out. After speaking with Ms. Harris on the phone, she said that I could drive over to her house to check out the basement. "Knock, knock" was the sound of my knuckles as they struck against Ms. Harris' front door after arriving on her porch. Minutes after checking out the basement, I told Ms. Harris that I will gladly rent out her basement by making a monthly payment of $250. She agreed and I moved in. Due to the need of finding employment because of relocating, I asked Ms. Harris if she knew of anyone who needed help. She informed me that a member of her church by the name of John Greer owned a landscaping business called Highly Favored and needed a driver to drive him around to the his worksites. After speaking with him and being informed that I wouldn't get paid much, I agreed that I would not only drive him to his worksites but also assist him with his landscaping duties as well so that I would be able to pay Ms. Harris for rent and provide food for myself.

Working for John was different from all of the other jobs that I worked before. I wasn't providing direct customer service to anyone this time around but instead performing manual labor. Even though it was very hot that summer and most of our work was performed outside, I learned to deal with it because I always reminded myself of the very first job that I had cutting grass with my great uncle in which I too had to work in the heat and was able to endure. During a conversation with John, he asked what I wanted to be in life. I told him that I was already involved in the Student Government Association and someday wanted to run for Student Body President and ultimately the President of the United States. He told me that I could do it if I came this far. And I replied, "I hope so."

John would also talk about Jesus Christ because he loved Christianity and was heavily involved in his church. Because he would often profess about Christianity while we worked, I became interested and wanted to know more about the religion. After all I learned a lot about it, he told me that at any time I wanted to accept the Lord Jesus Christ as my savior, let him know. Days passed after thinking long and hard about the offer. One day while we were working together, I told him that I wanted to give my life to Jesus Christ. Because I could not remember when or if I had already given it to him as a child, I officially gave it to him during the summer of 2010 after repeating the holy words after John.

I was very proud of myself because in order for me to have genuinely wanted to do this, I needed to truthfully understand the meaning of Christianity and its values which was a very mature phase that I had to undergo in my life. I would say that with all the sawing, tile lying, and construction work performed throughout the summer, I did learn a lot about landscaping and God. As I packed up to return to Raleigh, John told me to keep in touch with him so that he can stay abreast of all of my future goals and accomplishments.

Bound to start my second semester sophomore year, I began to map out my remaining goals to accomplish for undergraduate school. I also began working part-time at Chick-Fil-A as a cashier to get some change in my pocket for gas and other necessities. Before Christmas break of 2010, Masac introduced me to his close friend, Kevin Johnson. Kevin was from Baltimore, Maryland and was known by many of the ladies on campus to have a nice heart. Once he found out about my story, he offered that I come live with him and took me in as his brother to make sure I felt right at home.

After having another successful semester, I went in my fourth semester full throttle. During the spring, I received an unexpected email from the National Association for the Education of Homeless Children and Youth to attend its first LeTendre class reunion that would be held in my hometown, Washington, D.C. This was something that the scholars and I wished to happen before our departure back in 2009 in Denver, Colorado and for us to be the first class out of many of LeTendre classes to attend the reunion, it was definitely exciting. Reuniting with the others was awesome because we hadn't seen each other in two years. After sharing updates with one another, we noticed that some of us were living better lives while others' lives were getting worse. Because we viewed one another as brothers and sisters, we had to remind ourselves of how far we've come and how far we wanted to go which was to become successful despite our challenging past.

Although the stay in my hometown was nothing new to me because it was where I grew up, the others were impressed and fascinated because some of them thought that D.C. was only the home of the President of the U.S. and nothing else. During the reunion, we ate at restaurants such as Mad Hatter Grille, Hard Rock Café, and other great spots. However, the real reason why we were here was to help NAEHCY draft a Homeless Youth Act to congress. With our similar backgrounds, we were able to sit on Capitol Hill and have policy-makers from all 50 states listen to our stories to help lessen youth homelessness in the nation. This is where I also met another mentor named Matt Aronson. Matt was a new member of Sasha Bruce Youthwork and cared a lot about helping people like myself. Matt would call and check on me to see if I needed any money for food and other necessities while I was in school. He would always ask me to create a spreadsheet of all of the things that I will need for the academic school year such as ink pens, pencils, tablets, and other school supplies geared towards education so that he could work with Sasha Bruce Youthwork to obtain them for me.

Before the scholars and I left Capitol Hill, we all received an award from the United States Interagency Council on Homelessness for our efforts and courage to help others just like us. As the reunion came to a close, we made sure that all of us kept in touch by creating a special Facebook page, "Together As One...Our Way...Our Family" to help each other stay on the right path.

After touching back down in North Carolina, Kevin and I moved into a house with two other roommates, Marcus Kennedy and Glenn Jackson. Because the both of them attended our school, it was easier to manage paying the bills due to the trust we had amongst one another. This was a critical summer for me because I was becoming more exposed to adulthood by paying rent and taking care of other responsibilities. I also went from a guy who used to wear rundown shoes and cheap clothing handed down from donors and thrift shops, to the coolest and freshest student on campus wearing the most expensive shoes such as Nike Foamposites, Lebrons, True Religion Jeans, Hollister, Polo, and other name brand clothing thanks to the help of my roommates. This transition was very different for me because the students always had known me to walk around campus wearing bow ties and suspenders which was a unique style of dress to the other students on campus.

Because I had not been in contact with any of my family members due to me ending up homeless, I decided to search online to at least try to locate them but nothing surfaced. Not knowing my sister's whereabouts or if they were alive or dead, I prayed at night to God that my family was doing better than ever before and that they all had better lives.

Earning the Victory

As the fall semester arrived, I began to plan my junior year. After serving two years in the Student Government Association, I knew that I wanted to someday run for the President of the Association. For this reason, I had to start planning my campaign strategy effectively. After placing my name on the ballot against three other students for that academic year, I got right down to business. The rules were that we could begin campaigning against one another at the start of 12 midnight for two weeks. As soon as 12 midnight struck, I pulled out the campaign flyers that I made weeks before and posted them in every residence hall and corridor inside and outside of the classrooms. Later the same day, I ran down to FeDex Kinkos to have business cards made and knocked on each door in the residence halls to make sure that the students had my card and heard my pitch for why I wanted to serve as their President.

The platform that I chose was, "Together, if we believe, we can achieve." Days after thinking long and hard on what I wanted my platform to be, this one felt like the perfect choice. The platform was chosen because I never thought that I could leave a homeless shelter and go off to college as a teenager. But I did because I believed in the dream and if I had not believed in it, I would have never achieved it. Because of this, I wanted the concept to be similar for my campus to show that if the students believed that they could strengthen one another academically and socially, that they could achieve just that to make our school a better place.

Weeks into the campaign, I worked diligently as I passed out ice-cold water to students on hot days while my running mates did exactly nothing. One of them posted their flyers a couple days before students marched to the polls to vote when we were given a whole two weeks to campaign prior to that. Another candidate attached dollar bills to his business cards thinking that it would help give him the advantage. Huffing and puffing I walked into the classroom with my shirt drenched in sweat hours after campaigning under the hot blazing sun. Most of the students saw the hard work and dedication that I was putting in by giving me high fives and yelling, "Vote for Ant Ross!" in the hallways. As my campaign began to come to a close, it was time for me to deliver my candidacy speech to the student body. During our candidacy speeches, the sky turned gray and began to darken in threat of rain. Unfortunately, I was the last candidate to speak. Before I could rest my hands on the podium, rain started crashing down and I started to lose my audience because the speeches were held outside. Due to the terrible weather, the Director of Student Activities informed me that I would have my opportunity to speak at the last Ms. Saint Augustine's College pageant months before the school's name changed to Saint Augustine's University.

On the night of the pageant, I patiently sat and waited until it was my time to share the goals and future plans that I had in store for the student body. However, the hosts of the pageant forgot that I was scheduled to speak that night, lifted the lights, and concluded the pageant. Thinking quickly on my feet, I ran out the auditorium to gather everyone letting them know that I still did not give my candidacy speech and to come back inside. Everyone returned to the auditorium and took their seat. During my speech, I could hear people in awe after they heard about my struggle of homelessness and the extracurricular involvement and academic accomplishments I conquered despite my challenging past. After my speech, I received a standing ovation from the crowd with everyone saying, "Together, if we believe, we can achieve!" I received pats on my back as I was leaving the auditorium and received thanks from others for inspiring them because of all that I have done.

The next day, it was time for everyone to cast their votes. After the positive praise that I received throughout my campaign, I felt certain that I was going to win. After the Board of Elections tallied the votes, the results posted the morning after. Prayerfully, I walked into the Department of Student Affairs to read the results. "A four-way tie?!" I said aloud in confusion and disappointment. I went to the Dean of Students and asked, "How is it a four-way tie and it was only four of us running for the position?" With him replying that he didn't know, I knew deep down inside that I had just been cheated and that the system was rigged. I thought of this type of foul play because my running mates had no prior experience in the SGA and barely campaigned. They barely campaigned because they all belonged to either a fraternity or sorority and believed that they could win due to the popularity that they had on campus. Even the majority of the student body was shocked and disappointed by the outcome and expressed their concern to me by telling me to remain strong and that they'll vote for me again.

Even though my name remained on the ballot for a revote, I wanted to give up. I didn't want to campaign all over again because of the amount of hard work that I put into it the first time. I was angered and hurt because I put my heart into wanting nothing but the best for my campus. As the weekend passed, I spoke to some of my mentors about the situation. They told me that nothing was guaranteed in the world and that some of things that we desire do not come easy. They all ended the conversation with a similar question asking if I was going to sulk in defeat.

Monday arrived and with that same question running in my head, I jumped out of the bed, got dressed, and turned on my campaign mode. This time, I went even harder. I went table by table in the cafeteria during lunch and dinner informing the students that we all were tied and that I needed their votes once more. Puzzled and supportive at the same time, the students went to go cast their votes once again. Because of the rain on that day, I was concerned that fewer students would get out and vote. After the votes were tallied, results were posted on the bulletin board the following morning. Hoping that I had won, I pumped my fist in the air as I read my name confirming that I just came out victorious as the Student Body President of my college. This is where I had "earned" the victory. I was elated and grateful that all of my hard work had finally paid off and that the students chose me to lead them. Had I not come to my senses, given up, and sulked in defeat, I probably would not have won.

I would say that the beginning of my term was rough for me because I was "rolling with the big boys" as they called it. I sat on Executive Boards and made critical decisions for the student body to help better the campus. I learned more about politics and oversaw a budget that consisted over $15,000 for the academic year to host enrichment programs. Because everyone noticed my hard work and dedication, a lot of the students wanted to be involved in the association. I started with a cabinet of 16 members and ended with over 60 members dedicated to serving their campus community.

As SGA President, I spearheaded several programs such as registering hundreds of students to vote for upcoming local and state elections, diversified the cafeteria's menu, proposed a resolution to extend cafeteria seating, created a two-part "Go Green" initiative to help prevent and eliminate damage to the environment, and hosted events to help enhance the writing and literacy skills of the student body. My term as president was coined as, "One of the best Student Government Associations to grace the college's campus" by former SGA Presidents and previous members. And out of all of the student organizations on campus, we won the Student Program of the Year award by hosting over 48 campus-wide programs and having the most participants for events all year around. I also was later elected to serve as the Vice President of the Alpha Alpha Chapter of Alpha Kappa Mu National Honor Society and in the spring of 2012 I won the department award out of all of the political science majors at the university.

On one early foggy Sunday morning, I heard someone knocking at my door. After I opened the door, the Director of my residence hall, Mr. Khary Wright, handed me a piece of paper, told me to respond as soon as possible, and turned his back and walked away. Mr. Wright was a mentor who was loved by many of the students on campus. Whenever any of us had issues, we would go and visit him for advice. Mr. Wright was also amongst the few who gave me a place to stay during school breaks as well. After reading the paper that he handed me, I noticed the freemasonry logo printed on it. As I took a closer look, it was in fact an application to join the Scottish Rites Ancient Free and Accepted Masonry order as an Entered Apprentice. Because the local freemasonry chapter had a great reputation of providing service to their communities, I researched more about the organization. After reading all of what the brotherhood stood for, I decided to complete the application. I knew that I always wanted to join a brotherhood but I didn't know it to be this one. After I accepted the offer, Mr. Wright brought me on board. With becoming a member of the organization, I was able to view life differently when it came to coming to the aid of others in times of despair and providing service to the less fortunate. I would say that I had a lot of fun and enjoyed the times spent with my new fraternity brothers.

In the spring of 2012, I served as an intern for the youngest District Court Judge in Wake County appointed by the governor of North Carolina, Judge Vince Rozier. For the entire semester, Judge Rozier taught me the fundamentals of the judicial system and how it operated. I also observed trials from criminal, civil, family, and juvenile court to gain a deeper understanding of how the law is applied.

As my term as Student Body President began to come to a close, a lot of people mandated that I run for a second term. My response was that I had accomplished all that I needed to as president and would need to focus more on preparing for law school.

Harvard Law School

During the summer of 2012, I enrolled into a Law School Admissions Test (LSAT) prep course at N.C. State University for $1,000 after earning a B out of the class I took on my campus. I wanted to take the LSAT fully prepared and knowledgeable about its content. I also knew that I wanted to apply to Harvard University when I first saw it listed in the book of college and universities that Ms. Ebony sat on my lap during my visit to College Bound but did not meet the requirements to do so at the time because the school didn't accept G.E.D's. However, since I was about to earn my Bachelors of Arts degree, I would then be eligible to do so. For this reason, Harvard Law School was one of the schools that I knew I would apply to when the time came. Studying diligently from three different LSAT prep books throughout the summer, I was scheduled to take the test in October.

The night before the exam, I packed a small healthy breakfast, sharpened my No. 2 pencils, and took a good night's rest. Waking up the next morning refreshed and focused, I went in the exam center with confidence. "You may begin." the proctor stated as I turned my test booklet to the first section carefully reading the directions. Minutes into the exam, "You now have five minutes remaining" the proctor calmly stated prompting me to look over my work to make sure that I did not leave anything blank. After the exam was finished, I took a deep breath thanking God that it was finally over. As I awaited the results, I wanted to make sure that I finished my senior year off strong by doing all of the extra credit work that I could possibly do.

Before Christmas break, I was invited to live with a Jewish family named the Adelmans whom I met through community organizing that year. They took me in not only because of my story, but also because they told me about this guy named Dr. Norman who always looked out for them while they were in college and they wanted me to do the same when I was able to for others. This family truly wanted nothing from me but for me to "pay it forward" and do positive things in the world to help others unlike the other families that I lived with. While living with the Adelmans, I was exposed to the Jewish religion and its values. They would sing Jewish songs before meals and always ate kosher and organic foods. Although this was all new to me, it felt as if I was right at home.

Knowing that I just applied to one of the top schools in the world, I thought about it every time I was in the shower. I would fantasize walking on Harvard's campus in the snow and seeing myself wearing a hoody that read "Harvard Law School" on it. Months after taking the LSAT, my results finally arrived via email. Nervously, I opened the email to find that I scored only in the average percentile. After informing my mentors of the unexpected results, they told me that the LSAT was only one component of the application in gaining admission and that the other parts of my application would have to be reviewed as well. Knowing that I didn't obtain the test scores Harvard were looking for, others told me to remain optimistic and that if Harvard did not accept me that one of the other schools that I applied to might. Because I had a strong personal statement, had great extracurricular participation, inducted into multiple honor societies, was on the President's and Dean's list since freshmen year, had a 3.7 GPA on a 4.0 scale, and outstanding recommendation letters from notable people, I kept my head held high in confidence believing that I would attend someone's law school in the fall.

As months passed, the day finally arrived; the day that I received confirmation via email that I was not in fact moving to Cambridge, Massachusetts to attend Harvard Law School because I was denied admission. My body started to crumble inside as I read the letter that read:

Anthony D. Ross

"Dear Mr. Ross:

I regret to inform you that after careful consideration of your application, the Admissions Committee is unable to offer you admission to Harvard Law School. This year we received a large number of applications from an exceptionally well-qualified group of men and women, and we have to turn away many outstanding candidates.

During this admission season, over 5,000 applicants are applying for a limited number of spots in our entering class. There are many excellent law schools in the United States, and this denial of admission to Harvard Law School is not a negative estimation of your potential to study law nor should you allow it to be a judgment of your achievements. It is only the result of having many attractive candidates for comparatively few spaces in our class.

I want to thank you for your interest in Harvard Law School. I hope that you will accept my sincerest wishes for your future endeavors."

Sincerely,

The Admissions Committee"

I no longer wanted to live anymore after I received the bad news. It felt as if I had no reason to live anymore. Days after, my close friends, supporters, and mentors reminded me the need to keep my head up because it wasn't the end. They explained to me that Harvard wasn't the only law school in the world and that other law schools would be happy to have me. Weeks later, I received a letter in my mailbox from North Carolina Central University School of Law. NCCU was one out of many of the schools I applied to and also the first law school for African American students in North Carolina.

After opening the letter, it read that I was selected to attend one of their summer law programs. The purpose of the program was to expose prospective law students to the rigors of law school and help enhance our strategic and critical thinking skills to help us become successful as we matriculate. I was super excited because I really wanted to see what the program was about and wanted to get a feel for the professors and course work. As my senior year started to come to a close, I realized how much I grew and matured from the time that I was a teenager in the shelter back in D.C. to now. I learned a lot not only from my professors, but about life as a whole. It was a crazy feeling to know that I was about to walk across the stage in weeks with the same GPA that the girl in the shelter had that I was vying for; it was a major coincidence. I was later inducted into Pi Gamma Mu International Honor Society of Social Sciences where I was recognized for my academic achievements throughout my collegiate career.

Weeks before graduation, I posted my graduation invitation on social media networks such as Facebook and Instagram urging people to repost and share the invitation to help me find my family before graduation. After my invitation caught the attention of over 100,000 people worldwide through the social media outlets from everyone reposting and sharing, my family still did not surface. Thousands across the world continued to spread the word and wished me luck in my search while others asked to attend my graduation and give me gifts.

As graduation day grew closer, I started to get chills knowing that I was about to fulfill my dream of being homeless at age 13 to a college graduate. Hundreds of different family members belonging to the class of 2013 filled the crowd as they stood in line to take their seats on graduation day. Although some of the people who played an instrumental role in my success planned to attend, I was still nervous because I didn't know if my family, who I hadn't seen in years, would surprise me on this day and attend the ceremony as well.

Marching down the aisles dressed in my cap and gown wearing different colored honor cords representing many of the honor societies that I was inducted in, the political science medal around my neck beamed through the crowd as we walked to take our seats as the crowd cheered us on. As I looked around to see the familiar faces of my mentors and supporters in the crowd yelling in excitement, my anxiety grew even closer as the names of students were called one-by-one from each department to obtain their baton and undergraduate degree. Standing on a set of stairs leading up to the platform, I could hear majority of the crowd shouting in praise as I began to walk across the stage to shake hands with the chancellor and obtain my Bachelors of Arts degree in Political Science. With the biggest and brightest smile you have ever seen on a person's face, I received accolades from people from all over the campus who wanted to take pictures with me. It all felt surreal and simply mind blowing.

I not only graduated from Saint Augustine's University with Great Honor (Magna Cum Laude) but I also graduated in the top percentile of my class and department for which I was truly amazed. As I navigated through the crowd, I still did not see any of my family members. "How could this possibly be?" I asked myself after having thousands help search for their existence. Later that day, close to 20 people joined me at my graduation dinner celebration at P.F. Chang's China Bistro. Those in attendance were a mixture of my mentors and caseworkers from the group home that I left back in 2009. Paul, Mr. Antoine, Mr. George, Matt, Ms. Ebony, and many others sat with smiles on their faces as I passed around my degree. While opening my graduation gifts at the table, I still was a little saddened because I did not see any of my family members attend the ceremony. However, I had to believe that everything happened for a reason and that God placed the people who helped me in my life for a reason.

After photos of me holding my degree at graduation surfaced on the internet, it triggered thousands of shares and reposts on Facebook and Instagram generating thousands of comments and had close to 80,000 people across the world request to follow me on Instagram. Who knew that by me sharing my story on a social network would help inspire so many people across the world?

Weeks after graduation, my story reached my long-lost cousin's Facebook page on my grandfather's side. She messaged me and told me that she had recognized my face from the last time she saw me which was when I was at age five and that she was concerned about why she never heard from me again since then. However, she told me that after reading my story, she understood why. She then called my grandfather and informed him about my well-being. After I spoke to my grandfather, he passed my number along to my oldest sister so that we could reconnect. After speaking to her, I could hear the excitement from her voice and wanting to be in my life once again. Since then, I was able to reconnect with my other sisters due to the role that everyone across the world played with the power of social media. However, I have not been in touch with our mother since we were separated. Only time will tell to see if her and I will reconnect in this lifetime to see her son in the flesh as an accomplished and successful young man.

After being urged by so many people across the world to write a book, I did so in hopes of helping you all become successful despite your daily struggles. Everyone has a story; even you. You read time and time again of me being knocked down by this thing called "Life" even when I thought the struggle was over at times. You saw that I was rejected from my family as a child and rejected from my dream school. However, I did not quit! With the help of many individuals who wanted to see me soar for excellence, I was able to chase my dreams to no limit. Never let anyone tell you what you can do. I would not be here if it was not for God.

"Life's struggles are only temporary battles and we all are here to help each other get through them because it is impossible to face life alone. I hope that this book inspired you so that you can inspire the next generation. Who knows if I would ever live to see the day that I obtain my Jurist Doctorate degree from law school and someday fulfill my dream of becoming the President of the United States of America? Just know that I wrote this book for you; for you to conquer your dreams regardless of any obstacle standing in your way. Be it a pilot, entrepreneur, CEO, hair stylist, doctor, professional athlete, actress, singer, or anything else you dream of becoming, you can accomplish it only if you believe that you can achieve." –Anthony D. Ross

Pictured is when I was a guest speaker at the British Embassy. From left to right: The British Ambassador Sir Nigel Sheinwald, the former Mayor of Washington, DC, Adrian Fenty, the Mayor's Wife, Me, world renowned opera singer, Denise Graves and her husband, along with the British Ambassador's wife.

The photo that I snapped from my window seat during my FIRST plane ride ever en route to Denver, Colorado.

The LeTendre Scholars Class of 2009 from the National Association for the Education of Homeless Children and Youth.

When we went on Capitol Hill to help draft the Homeless Youth Act to Congress in the summer of 2011.

The night that I was sworn in as Student Body President of my University my junior year for the (2011-2012) academic school year.

The Student Government Association cleaning the cafeteria and implementing one of our "Go Green" initiatives.

The boys and I from the Cornel West Academy of Excellence

The Adelmans and I

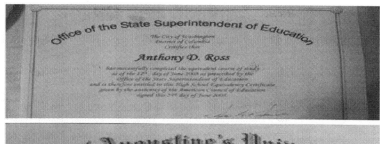

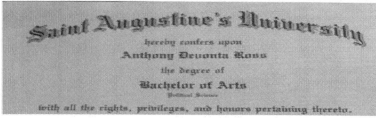

When I went from earning a G.E.D. to a Bachelors of Arts degree in Political Science

All of the awards and honors that I brought back to the homeless shelter that I grew up in before I went off to college. The U.S. seal in the middle is the award that I received from the United States Interagency Council on Homelessness.

The graduation invitation that I posted on Facebook and Instagram that thousands of people across the world shared and reposted to help me find my family before graduation.

Graduation Day

From the top left to right: Mr. George and his coworker, my friend's dad, Mr. Antoine's wife, Paul Brunson holding his son Kingston, Andre Smith, Paul's wife, Ms. Ebony Lea, Mr. Antoine Medley, Danyelle Villilines, and my friends and I from school.

Paul and I

The End

94075091R00054

Made in the USA
Columbia, SC
25 April 2018